Stock Market Investing for Beginners

The Ultimate Guide to Creating a Profitable Portfolio

Gualtiero Favole

Table of Contents

Introduction

Welcome to *"Stock Market Investing for Beginners. The Ultimate Guide to Creating a Profitable Portfolio."* This is the beginning of an exciting journey that will lead you to become financially independent. In the following pages, you will uncover the secrets the stock traders and financial experts know but don't want to share with you. Herein, you'll find a treasure trove of insider secrets. If you believe there is a magic formula for making money investing in stock, you'll find that all it takes is the right know-how.

Throughout this book, we will discuss the information you need to know. We will dispense with the fluff and focus on the meat and potatoes. You will get the real information on how to make money, thereby creating a solid financial life for you and your family.

We are going to delve into the secrets of day trading. If you are keen on rolling up your sleeves, day trading is the right approach for you. You'll find out how you can make money day trading, from the comfort of your home and office, and without having to work more than you already do.

We are also going to look into swing trading. This trading approach is highly profitable. However, you need to know when to strike. In doing so, you'll be able to cash in on market opportunities that don't come around very often. But when they do, you will be ready for them.

We are going to discuss position trading. This is a long-term trading strategy that will allow you to maximize your returns. This is where you hit home runs. They take time to set up. But once you have the right deal in place, it can be very rewarding for you. As such, position trading is the ultimate approach for high-value investors.

If this sounds too good to be true, then stick around to learn how you can make the most of your time and effort. You are surely interested in investing as you are looking for the best way to help your family be financially secure.

You can't guarantee your family's financial wellbeing by taking on another job. Nor can you become financially independent by working longer hours. This is the reason why stock investing is so appealing. Plenty of other folks out there have made stock investing work for them. Now, it's your turn to make some real money.

Ultimately, you can continue to live your usual life knowing that you have all of your bases covered. You can afford to continue your day job, not because you have to, but because you want. This is the type of freedom that can come from stock market investing.

The secrets are here.

Once you see them in action, you will realize that it's simple to achieve. However, the right know-how is essential to making things work for you. So, buckle up because we are going to cover a lot of information. Rest assured that the information we will discuss is presented in a clear and concise form.

Thanks again for choosing this book, make sure to leave a short review on Amazon if you enjoy it, i'd really love to hear your thoughts!

Let' get down to business!

Chapter 1: Why Should You Invest?

To invest, or not invest? That is the question.

When you think about investing, what comes to mind?

For most people, the idea of investing is very similar to gambling. They roll the dice on a stock, win big, and solve all of their problems. However, this is something seen in the movies but not in real life. In real life, investing is a carefully planned action. By taking the time to carefully plan investments, returns are often much greater than expected.

Therefore, investing is something that we need to see as an opportunity. If you look at investing as pain today, fun tomorrow, then you will never make it. When you commit to investing because you know you will achieve your objectives, then you are well on your way to making some serious cash.

So, let's take a look at the reason why you should invest.

Make Extra Income

The majority of folks that invest do so to supplement their current income. It's hard to make a decent living from just one income stream. Moreover, it's hard to make money by working longer hours. Therefore, most people look for other means of supplementing their monthly income.

This is where investing comes into play.

When you invest money, you eventually get paid returns on your investments. Typical investment vehicles such as mutual and index funds pay interest on a monthly or quarterly basis. They provide additional funds that can be put toward any number of purposes. However, the returns you can get from these investments are often underwhelming.

Many times, the returns you get from mutual funds can be disappointing. This is the reason why lots of people look toward investing directly into stocks. By cutting out middlemen, investors stand to make far better gains. As such, savvy, proactive investors use day, swing, and position trading as a way of generating regular income. When you come to combine your regular income plus income from investing, you have a winning formula that can help you fund a comfortable lifestyle.

Planning for Retirement

This is a long-term approach. Investment accounts such as IRAs and 401(k)s provide a way of financing expenses during retirement years. These investments work very well for folks who have time to spare. Thus, the younger you get started, the more money you stand to make. By the same token, the longer you take to open one of these accounts, the less time you have to fund your retirement.

Therefore, investing in stocks makes sense for those looking to save up for retirement. Depending on your strategy, you can simply roll over investment to make your nest egg grow. Over time, you'll not only have a regular income but also a substantial amount of capital racked up. As a result, stock investing makes perfect sense for those saving up for retirement.

Earn Passive Income

Passive income is one of the most intriguing reasons to invest. Passive income basically means you don't actively work for the income you earn. This may sound too good to be true, but it is a fact. When you invest in stocks, you can set up your trading system to do the work for you. Nowadays, virtually all trading is done through computers. There is algorithmic trading you can use to help you automate all of your transactions. Consequently, all you need to do is set up your trades and let the system handle the rest.

By taking advantage of automated trading, you can devote a couple of hours a day, or a week even, to your trades. Once you have everything set up, you can sit back and watch the action. Of course, you need to stay on top of the action. But doing so won't require you to spend hours in front of the computer.

Also, there are folks who choose to make trading a full-time job. If you choose to do so, you can work both actively and passively. You can set up trades to work automatically while you focus on other directly. In a way, you are conducting multiple trades at once.

If you have ever wondered how stockbrokers make so much money in a short time frame, this is the answer. They use the power of automated trading to do multiple transactions at once.

Achieve Financial Independence

Financial independence means that you don't need to work to finance your lifestyle. In other words, you choose to work. You work because you want to, not because you have to. This is the true meaning of freedom. Additionally, this is not something that you can achieve by working a job.

People who become financially independent achieve this by investing in stocks, real estate, or business ventures. They reach a point where they have regular income without actively working. Therefore, they don't need to work a 9 to 5 routine to make money. They have an automated system that works for them.

When you achieve financial independence, you can afford to make time for the things you have always wanted. You can provide for your loved ones without having to sacrifice your time. You can prioritize your health rather than work. In the end, financial independence is the ultimate goal most people seek.

The truth is that most people say they want to be rich. What they mean is that they don't want to worry about paying the bills every month. What most people really want is to have a comfortable life in which they can afford to do whatever they want, whenever they want. Thus, they are not obsessed with a specific amount of money in their bank account.

Now, if you are keen on becoming truly wealthy, then you can certainly achieve this through stock investing. It takes time and patience, but it pays off in the end. The principles in this book will help you get there. But you need to start investing today. The longer you wait, the longer it will take you to get to the promised land.

Chapter 2:
Fundamentals of Stock Market Investing

To be successful in the stock market, you need to understand the nuts and bolts that hold it together. Generally speaking, the stock market functions like any other market. There are buyers and sellers that come together to agree on a price. As such, price is the ultimate mechanism by which investors can carry out transactions.

So, let's discuss how the market prices stocks.

How to Price Stocks

The core element of pricing stocks is supply and demand. In short, when there is high demand (lots of buyers) and low supply (few sellers), then price goes up. In contrast, when there is low demand (few sellers) and high supply (lots of sellers), price goes down. If sellers and buyers are equal, then there is a perfect market price. This is the general rule that's applied to all commodities in a free market. Unless a market is manipulated, supply and demand will determine the bulk of price action.

However, there are additional factors that determine pricing in financial markets. The main factor is psychological. By "psychological" we mean what investors believe may or may not happen. For instance, if investors feel that a specific company is undervalued, they will flock to buy it up. As such, their desire to own this company's stock will cause the price to go up. By the same token, if investors feel there is something wrong with a company, its stock price will plummet.

Also, economic conditions may lead investors to think twice about buying and/or selling. For example, during a recession, investors may be far more cautious. After all, they might be concerned about the long-term effects of the current economic outlook.

Furthermore, company financials, management, and competition play a significant role in its stock valuation. If a company has solid financials, reputable management, and is at the top of its industry, then you have a winner. However, don't be surprised to hear an investor bet on long shots. These are companies that are unproven, or might be poised for a turnaround after a tough spell. However, always be careful with betting on long shots. There is never any guarantee they will play out.

Looking to the Future

To look into the future, you need to look into the past. With stock prices, you can glean into the future by looking at the history of price action. Individual companies all have historical data on the behavior of its market valuation. This information allows you to look toward the future. From its past trend, you can figure out what might happen. Of course, nothing is certain. Still, you may be able to get a good picture of the future.

Therefore, you must become familiar with charts and graphs. These elements are the graphic representation of the data pertaining to price action. The most common graph is a line graph. Line graphs are perfect at showing the behavior of a stock's trend. Moreover, it will enable you to get a sense of what will happen by its patterns.

The study of quantitative data is called "technical analysis." Technical analysis is crucial to making informed decisions. If you make investment decisions based on your subjective appreciation, then you are basically guessing. As such, you must have objective data to make reasonable assumptions on a stock. Otherwise, the risk of losing on a deal grows exponentially.

Market Organization

When you hear about the "stock market," what you are really hearing about is the collection of stock exchanges located throughout the world. A stock exchange is a physical location in which buyers and sellers of financial assets come together. The most famous stock exchange in the world is the New York Stock Exchange located on Wall Street in New York City. This is the place where the bulk of the transactions happen in the United States. Nevertheless, there are similar exchanges in Philadelphia, Chicago, and Miami.

Additionally, there are a number of stock exchanges around the world. Some of the largest are located in European cities such as London, Paris, Frankfurt, and Madrid. In Asia, the most predominant stock exchanges can be found in Shanghai, Tokyo, and Seoul. There are other markets in Latin America, as well.

When you buy and sell stocks, among other assets, you trade directly in one of these stock exchanges. As a result, you must become familiar with the various kinds of assets trade in them. Please keep in mind that you won't always find the same assets in all markets. Some markets specialize in one type of asset over another. Moreover, companies are listed on a single exchange. Thus, a company that is listed in the United States cannot be listed in another country. So, if you are keen on trading specific companies, you might have to look at an overseas market, as well.

Asset Classes

Stocks are not the only assets that are traded in financial markets. There are a plethora of assets to choose from. In this book, we're focusing on stocks. Nevertheless, here is a list of the assets you can trade in financial markets:

- Government bonds (both US and other countries)

- Commodities (agricultural products, cattle, precious metals, industrial metals, energy)

- Currencies (any currency in the world)

- Derivatives (futures, swaps, options)

- Funds (mutual, index, exchange-traded)

These asset classes have a number of instruments you can buy and sell. Some are great for a "buy and hold" strategy, like bonds, while others are better for short-term investments such as commodities. Ultimately, you can choose to invest in any of these asset classes based on your expectations and your goals.

We recommend starting out with stock. It is the best way to get started before branching out into other asset classes. Since some transactions require a greater amount of experience and study, it is important to master stock trading before taking the plunge into other asset classes. Still, you can build a diversified portfolio by investing in various asset classes. Diversification is a great strategy especially when you are looking to protect yourself against long-term risk.

Chapter 3: How to Create an Investment Timeline

Creating an investment timeline is all about managing your expectations. When you are keenly aware of the potential in the market, it is easy to get caught up in the excitement. Many investors engage in wishful thinking. They believe they can score a huge deal that will solve all of their problems.

This is something that you'd only see in the movies.

While it is possible to knock one out of the park, doing so requires time and research. If you can spot a deal like this, you might be poised to clean up. Otherwise, you may find yourself searching for the elusive "big one."

Managing Expectations

The most important part of managing expectations is being realistic. By "realistic" we mean understanding that it takes time to build a winning strategy. Therefore, you need to have patience in the early going. For instance, a realistic assumption would be to make a few hundred dollars in your first month of trading. It may not be enough to pay for all of your expenses, but it would be a welcome windfall.

It is practically impossible to indicate a specific sum of money you could make in your first few weeks of trading. Depending on your strategy and starting capital, you could make anywhere from $200 to $300, to several thousand. However, it's also important to keep in mind that most investors lose money at first. By sticking to their game plan, they turn things around and make up lost ground.

Based on this, it is reasonable to assume that you will make enough money to supplement your monthly income in the early going. If you start with an investment capital such as a few hundred dollars, you might be able to turn that into $100 or more.

Here is a reasonable way of determining how much you could make based on your starting capital. Average market returns range between 5% to 10% annually. If you break it down, that's roughly 1% to 2% a month. That might not seem like a lot. But when you multiply it over the number of transactions and investment capital, you could potentially make a fair amount of money. Later on, we'll discuss the strategies that you can use to maximize your returns.

Most investors reach complete financial independence at different points in their lives. The easy answer is this: the simpler your lifestyle, the sooner you can become financially independent. Consequently, if you only need $1,500 a month to finance your lifestyle, you may get there in a couple of years, if not much sooner. In contrast, if you need $5,000 a month to fund your living expenses, then it might take you several years to get there. In the end, it all boils down to your overall lifestyle.

Determine the Lifestyle You Want

Speaking of lifestyles, having a clear idea of what your ideal lifestyle is, constitutes the backbone of your investment timeline. There is nothing wrong with dreaming big. However, it's important for you to know that financial independence is about financing your lifestyle without the need to work for an indefinite time frame. For some, "indefinite" might mean the rest of their lives. For others, it might just mean taking off as much time as they want.

To calculate how much money you need to finance your lifestyle, all you need is to crunch the numbers. Take your current lifestyle. Use it as a baseline. Add up all of your expenses in a month. Try your best to include everything you spend on. The greater the detail, the more accurate the number.

Now, let's assume your monthly number is $1,000. Thus, you would need to produce an income of $1,000 per month to finance your lifestyle. This is your baseline.

The next step is to figure out the lifestyle that you want. To calculate this number, you would need to figure out how much it would cost you to finance this type of life. You would need to add up all the expenses that would be involved and then come up with a number. So, let's assume that your ideal lifestyle would cost you $2,000. Hence, you would need to first produce $1,000 to achieve financial independence, but then produce $2,000 to get to your ideal lifestyle.

Calculating Financial Independence

To calculate how long it will take you to be financially independent is about consistently hitting the number you need to finance your lifestyle. When you can consistently make enough money to finance your lifestyle, you know you're there. So, if you are able to produce $1,000 (according to our example) for three consecutive months, then you know you have hit the mark.

Let's assume a 5% monthly return rate on your investment. So, to produce $1,000 in profits, you would need to invest $20,000 each month. A 5% return on $20,000 is $1,000. If you have $20,000 on hand at the moment, then generating this type of return will take you a couple of months. But if you are starting out with $1,000, then it will take you several months to achieve this type of return.

To come up with a fairly accurate number, let's take a 5% return on $1,000. That's $50. Next, roll over your profits plus investment capital. So, in month number two, you would invest $1,050. At a 5% return, month number two would yield $52.50. On month number three, you would invest $1,102.50.

In this example, we're using small numbers and assuming very conservative returns. Nevertheless, it illustrates the type of calculation you would need to make to reach your desired target. The main thing to keep in mind here is to resist the temptation to take out your profits during the first few months. If you can simply keep rolling over your investments every month, you'll build up your investment capital. Before you know it, you'll have a large capital to work with. This will make reaching your desired target much easier.

Chapter 4: How to Define Your Investment Strategy

Having an investment strategy is a fundamental aspect of successful stock market trading. Without it, you're essentially groping in the dark. While you may be very adept at technical analysis, you will find it hard to have a clear direction for your portfolio. Of course, you can still make money. However, you won't make the best return you could make.

It is important for you to determine what your game plan is going to be. When you have this plan worked out, you can then go about finding the stocks to match your aims. In this chapter, we are going to look at three great investment strategies you can use to make serious gains.

Buy and Hold

The "buy and hold" strategy is a long-term strategy. In this strategy, you buy up assets and hold on to them until their price shoots up. At that point, you can sell your holdings. Now, it should be noted that the definition of "long term" in stock trading is any time frame over a month. As such, you should expect to hold on to stocks for at least a month.

This strategy is great when you find undervalued stocks. For instance, companies that have great track records but have fallen on hard times. Oil companies are a great example of this. Oil companies have no fault in geopolitical issues that cause the price of oil to fall. Nevertheless, when the price of oil plummets, oil companies take serious hits.

To capitalize on this phenomenon, you buy up oil stocks when they sink. Then, you hold on to them until the price of oil rebounds. Thus, oil stocks rebound as well. In some cases, it might be a question of days. In other cases, it might be a question of weeks. Ultimately, you need to be on top of news and developments across various industries.

High-Frequency Trading

High-frequency trading, or HFT, is a staple of day traders. This is a very short-term strategy. It consists of making multiple trades over and over. You don't make a lot of money per trade with this strategy. However, when you multiply your gains over a large number of transactions, the profits add up.

To make this strategy work, you need to find a stock that is trading in a range. This means that they go up to a specific value and then back down to a certain value. Meanwhile, they don't typically deviate from these limits. As a result, you can fairly predict where the price action will be.

Many times, HFT traders make pennies per trade. But when the total number of trades is calculated, the results could add up to hundreds of dollars a day. Therefore, it is a good strategy to use while you execute the "buy and hold" with other stocks.

Also, HFT is great for investors who are starting with very little investment capital. As such, HFT traders move the same investment capital over and over again. For instance, the invest $1,000 over and over making profits on the same amount of money. In the end, they generate returns is if they had invested $100,000.

As a novice investor, you ought to consider HFT. It will require you to spend some time at your computer setting up deals. But once you get the hang of it, you can easily set everything up at the start of your day, and then sit back to take in all the action.

Value Investing

Value investing consists of finding undervalued stocks and holding them until they bounce back. Now, the main difference between value investing and the buy and hold strategy is that value investing looks to find companies that will rebound in a shorter time frame. In the case of the buy and hold, you are looking to hold stocks for over a month. In value investing, you're looking to hold stocks for days or a couple of weeks.

The trick to value investing is finding stocks that are poised to make a comeback sooner rather than later. To execute the value investing strategy, you need to look at a company's book value. The term "book value" refers to a company's share price based on its accounting. As such, a company's financials will tell you what their share price is really worth. Then, you must compare the company's book value with its market valuation. If you find that the company's market valuation is below its book value, then you have an undervalued company.

However, there is a catch.

When going about value investing, you must ensure that the company is not in serious trouble. Therefore, you need to do your homework carefully. In some cases, a company may be going through a temporary situation. This is not a reflection of poor management or bad financials. As such, you can assume the company will bounce back.

In value investing, things can happen very quickly. So, you need to be ready for the possible changes that may take place. Still, it is a very good strategy when you're looking for an intermediate step between the buy and hold and HFT.

Setting Objectives

The strategies mentioned in this chapter are all aligned to your objectives. Whether you're looking to supplement your monthly income or become a billionaire, you need to be clear on what you want to achieve. Then, you can align your strategy.

Generally speaking, novice investors start with HFT, then move up to value investing before using the buy and hold. Ultimately, you can combine all three strategies to keep your portfolio engaged in the short, medium, and long term. As such, you will gain exposure to all investment time frames.

This approach will help you make short-term gains while allowing you to cash in on the big trades that happen in the long term. This is the reason why it is so important for you to do your homework. Thus, the more informed you are, the easier it will be for you to make some serious returns.

Chapter 5: Fundamentals of Day Trading

To invest in stocks, you can go the usual route. So, you can buy mutual funds or pay a stockbroker to manage your portfolio. However, this route will only get you so far. You'll be quite surprised to find the potential returns to be quite underwhelming.

Because of underwhelming returns, many investors choose to go at it alone. This is the reason why they turn to day trading. In this chapter, we'll be looking at the fundamentals of day trading, and why it might be a good choice for you.

Definition of Day Trading

Day trading is a stock investing approach in which the investor takes full control of their portfolio. In other words, the investor decides what stocks to buy and sell. Moreover, the investor decides when to make trades happen.

By definition, day trading is a short-term trading approach. Investors open and close positions on the same trading day. Therefore, they start and end the day with a clean slate. The reason for this is simplicity. If you leave positions open overnight, you might become vulnerable to external factors. The result may be unexpected shifts in price action.

Therefore, investors seek to avoid becoming vulnerable by closing all of their positions at the end of the trading. As such, they cash out for the day. This is a highly practical approach as it enables investors to avoid dealing with possible price shocks that may occur at the start of the trading day.

Day trading is perfect for those investors who are starting out with relatively small investment capital and are looking to make short-term gains. For those investors with larger investment capital, day trading may be one part of their overall investment approach.

How to Get Started With Day Trading

To get started with day trading, you need a brokerage account. A brokerage account is an agreement that you enter with a financial institution. This institution is a duly license stock trading corporation. Hence, this corporation allows you to gain access to the market through the use of their trading platform. In short, you become a stockbroker yourself. The only downside is that you are solely responsible for anything that happens. So, if you lose all your money, you have no one to blame but yourself.

There are two main types of brokerage accounts. There is a "full service" account. This account type gives you all the bells and whistles. These accounts charge a sign-up fee in addition to transaction fees per trade. Yet, they provide you with real-time quotes and analytics. Also, they provide expert advice and recommendations. Thus, they facilitate the process of deciding where to allocate your funds.

The other type of account is a "discount" account. When you sign up with a discount broker, you mainly receive access to the trading platform but without the bells and whistles. Therefore, you need to figure out where you can get information on the stocks you wish to trade. The good thing about discount brokers is that they charge a one-time sign-up fee. They also have lower transaction fees per trade. Although, you would need to buy trade bundles as opposed to a pay-as-you-go strategy.

Once you sign up for a brokerage account, you are ready to trade. It is relatively straightforward. However, do keep in mind that brokerage accounts vary in conditions. Some may require you to have several thousand dollars' worth of investment capital while others may only require you to have as little as $500.

One very important thing to keep in mind is the free demo account. Any reputable brokerage firm will grant you free access to the platform via a demo account. In a demo account, you play the real game using monopoly money. As such, you are trading on the real platform, with real data and analytics, but not with real money. This is why a demo account is great. It allows you to test out your strategy before you go live with real trades. It affords you the opportunity to make mistakes without losing your shirt in the process.

The Best Day Trading Strategy

The best day trading strategy, especially for beginners, is HFT. HFT is quite easy to master. That is why HFT is the best strategy for new investors. Plus, it doesn't require a great deal of investment capital. If you sign up for a discount account, you can turn $500 into a fairly decent amount in a few weeks. Naturally, the more trades you make, the greater your chances of making your capital grow.

Early on, you ought to consider rolling over your profits. It is recommended that you resist the temptation of pulling out your winnings. The idea is to build up your investment capital so that it can produce even greater returns.

The only catch to HFT is transaction fees. Please make sure that you are perfectly aware of how much your broker charges per trade. It could be that high transaction fees zap your profits. To avoid getting hit with high transaction fees, it's a good idea to purchase bundles. For example, your broker may offer 10 trades for $2.99. This type of package allows you to calculate your cost, thereby enabling you to visualize your returns.

How to Determine if Day Trading Is for You

Naturally, day trading is not for everyone. To be successful, day trading requires a commitment to learning the trading platform. By learning the platform, you'll be able to set up all your deals appropriately. Then, you can let the platform do its job.

Day trading may not be right for you if you are looking to become a passive investor. As a passive investor, you are not keen on becoming actively involved in trading. Nevertheless, day trading can help you become a passive investor as it would only require you to go about setting up your deals at the outset of the trading day. By the end of the day, the system will close out your positions. Meanwhile, you can spend your time researching your next move.

Chapter 6: How to Succeed at Day Trading

When you go about day trading, it is essential to have strategies that you can use to help you make money most of the time. If you lack reliable go-to strategies, you may find yourself guessing about what to do. Thus, having a clear idea of what you can do at all times is the best way to get ahead in the game.

In this chapter, we are going to take a look at some core strategies to help you make money while also helping you get ahead of the game. Now, it's worth noting that most investors have a 50% to 60% success rate. In general, investors win most trades. However, please be prepared to lose. So, your strategy boils down to what you can do when things don't work out. Your reaction in these situations will enable you to become a highly successful investor.

Core Strategies

To be successful, you must follow these core strategies. They are cross-cutting recommendations that you can implement any time you choose to enter a trade. Moreover, these strategies are time-tested tactics that can keep you safe from the mistake novice investors make. Therefore, do keep them at the forefront of your mind as you engage in stock investing.

Money management

Money management refers to the way you manage your investment capital. This is an approach that you can use to help you develop discipline in your asset allocation. There are two main rules that you need to follow.

- **The golden rule**. This rule refers to limiting the amount of capital you sink into individual trades. The golden rule states that you must never invest more than 2% of your total investment capital into a single trade. While you can invest the full sum of your capital, you shouldn't invest it all in a single trade. Please keep in mind that the more money you sink into an individual trade, the greater the risk.

- **Doubling down**. When investors lose money, they are tempted to invest twice as much in the next trade to compensate for the loss in the previous one. This strategy is highly dangerous. It can lead you to lose twice as much as you did before. For example, if you lost $100 on a trade, you might be tempted to invest $200 in the one. However, if something goes wrong, you risk losing $200 on top of the original $100. So, it's best to simply follow your strategy. You'll eventually recoup your losses.

Timing the market

Generally speaking, the largest amount of trading activity happens at the beginning and end of the trading session. Therefore, these are the times when you need to jump into the fray. The first two hours of the trading day show a flurry of activity. Here, you can perfectly implement an HFT strategy. You can make multiple trades within a short two-hour window. Some traders open and close positions in a matter of seconds. The same goes for the last hour and a half prior to market closing. This is a perfect time to liquidate any open positions. However, you need to be careful as the market selloff right before the end of the day may cause you to take a cut on your profits.

Time Management

Time management is about being consistent. Investing time daily to develop your craft is ideal. If you only go over charts or look at your trading platform once or twice a week, you may be surprised to find that your results aren't what you expect them to be. As a result, being consistent in the amount of time you spend is key.

Most successful day traders spend about two to three hours a day on their trading platform in addition to any time they spend on research. If you have a full-service account, much of the research is done for you. So, all you have to do is go over your news feed to see where you want to place your trades. You can then set up the system to take care of everything for you.

Core Components

Every good strategy regardless of its structure must have the following three components. These components are always present. Therefore, you cannot ignore them. If you fail to acknowledge them, they'll come back to bite you. So, it's best to take care of them right away. Doing so will help you avoid a myriad of problems later on.

Liquidity

Liquidity refers to the ease you would have to buy and sell an asset. Some assets are highly liquid while others are not. This term refers to how easily you could sell something especially in times of turmoil. For example, a house is a great example of an illiquid asset. After all, you can't expect to sell a house in five minutes. It may take weeks, even months, before you get a good offer.

Highly liquid assets include desirable stocks (blue-chip companies like Apple, Facebook, or GM), commodities (gold, oil), or currencies. Depending on the nature of the asset, you may have offers already lined up. So, make sure to focus on liquid assets.

In contrast, illiquid assets may be highly profitable but hard to move during a market downturn. For instance, real estate, intellectual property, or industrial assets are all valuable but hard to find buyers. These assets are much better for a buy and hold strategy as opposed to a short-term one.

Volatility

Volatility refers to the amount of trading volume occurring at any point. For example, volatility picks up at the beginning of the trading day. This is a natural occurrence derived from the entry of all players into the game.

Volatility can also increase when there are unexpected events in the economy. These events can come in the form of government policy, natural disasters, or poor economic data. However, these events may also be positive. If they are positive events, volatility may pick up in terms of buying rather than selling.

When volatility is low, you may not have the chance to make significant gains. Therefore, an HFT approach is best. If volatility is high, you might find that undervalued companies may rise to the occasion. So, it's best to find undervalued companies before volatility picks up. Then, when volatility rises, you can sell amid the frenzy.

Volume

Volume refers to the number of times an individual has been traded during a specific time frame. Volume in an indication of how liquid a stock is. As such, the lower the volume, the less popular the stock is. Therefore, you might have trouble selling it in a short time window. In contrast, if a stock has a high trading volume, then you can confidently but it and sell it whenever you need to. This is the core indicator you need to look at when considering an individual stock for HFT.

Most Successful Day Trading Strategies

Let's take a look at the most successful day trading strategies. These strategies can help you make a great deal of money when executed correctly. In some cases, you can hit it out of the park. Please note that these strategies are not always suited for HFT. So, you may have to hold on to stocks for a few hours as opposed to a few minutes. Nevertheless, the profits can make up the difference.

1. **Breakout**

This strategy refers to stock breaking past a specific upper limit. A stock's upper limit is known as a "resistance level." This is a psychological barrier in which investors are unwilling to surpass. In other words, investors feel that this point makes the stock too expensive. However, there are times in which investors are waiting for an event before deciding to buy up the stock. For example, investors may be waiting for economic data from the government. If the data is positive, they jump in. If the data is bad, they will hold.

Entry point: To determine your entry point in this trade, take a look at the stock's price history. If you find that it was at a higher price point previously, you have a reference to where the price could land. The stock is poised to break out when you see its price hit the resistance level but not surpass it. After three successive hits on a resistance level, the stock may be ready to achieve a breakthrough. While the timing is unpredictable, indications are that it will happen very quickly. So, do keep this in mind.

Exit point: The exit point of your trade is any point above the resistance level. A good rule of thumb is to place your sell price at a reasonable level. For example, anything close to or at its previous high is a good idea. Unless there is reason to believe that the price will break past its previous highs, you are better off sticking to its previous high. Depending on your entry point, you could really make a killing.

2. **Reversal**

A reversal is when a stock's price is trending downward, levels off, and the rises. The opposite is also true. Therefore, reversals are highly useful as both entry and exit points. To execute this strategy, you need to be aware of the stock's price history. Based on this, you can determine if and when a reversal in trend will take place.

Let's consider a downward trend. This is also called a "bearish" trend. When there is a bearish trend, a stock's price will eventually fall to a specific point and then rebound. It can be quite difficult to predict the exact point in which it will happen. But with the use of technical analysis, you can spot the point in which trend is about to reverse.

To spot the reversal, you must look at the point in which the trendline stops falling and then flattens out. Then, you can see the point in which the trendline will begin to rise. Sometimes, the trendline will have a "V" shape. This means it falls, hits a point, and then bounces back up immediately. The point right before the price begins to rebound is your optimal entry point. Therefore, this is the lowest price you can buy before the stock begins to rise.

In the opposite scenario, you have a "bullish" trend. This type of trend means the price is rising to a point in which it will come back down. The point right before the price drops back down is your optimal sell point. As such, this is the point where you'll make the most profit.

When you use reversals, you can buy at the lowest possible point and then sell at the highest possible price. This is how you can maximize profits.

3. Momentum or piggybacking

In this strategy, you are "riding the wave." It is best executed when there is news that alters investors' perceptions. For example, a company announces better-than-expected earnings. So, as soon as you hear the news, you buy it. As the wave rises, you sell. This will help you make some quick profits. However, you need to be careful not to wait too long. In this strategy, investors want to rise to the highest part of the wave. The problem is that waiting too long may set you up for a precipitous crash. In the best of cases, you'd see your profits reduced. In the worst of cases, you might end up losing money on the deal. Therefore, piggybacking is about entering quickly, making a profit, and then pulling out. It is a very short-term strategy. Thus, you must be ready to act quickly. Riding on momentum is relatively predictable especially during earnings season. It's a perfect way to make some quick funds during moments of increased volatility and volume.

The same can also be done when a stock pulls back. Often, stocks drop in price right before rising. This is commonly referred to as "buying on the dip." This strategy allows for short-term gains especially when there is a high degree of volatility. So, keep your eyes open for these movements. They can prove to be quite profitable in the short term.

Chapter 7: Fundamentals of Swing Trading

Swing trading is another approach investors use to maximize profits. This approach calls for more patience as investors are looking toward a longer time frame. As such, swing trading goes beyond the one-day time frame of day trading. With swing trading, investors hold open positions for periods ranging from a few days to several weeks.

The main purpose of swing trading is to capitalize on market "swings." Since we're looking at a longer time frame, we're anticipating much larger swings in price action. Instead of focusing on price action that shifts in pennies, we're anticipating much larger swings. Depending on the size of a position, this could represent hundreds, if not thousands of dollars.

Difference Between Day and Swing Trading

On the whole, day and swing trading work in the same way. The same type of trading platform is used. Also, the same techniques and analytical tools are used. The main difference lies in the time frame in which trades are placed. Day trading calls for opening and closing positions within the same trading session. In swing trading, you need to be prepared to keep your positions open for a much longer time frame. However, this is how you maximize profit.

Another important difference lies in the use of risk/reward ratios. In essence, a risk/reward ratio is based upon a potential loss versus a potential gain. Naturally, if the gain outweighs the loss, then the deal is worth entering. For instance, a good rule of thumb is a 3:1 risk to reward ratio. In other words, you stand to make $3 while risking a loss of $1. In the case of day trading, risk to reward ratios doesn't make much sense as the trade is so short-term.

It's also worth mentioning that swing trading requires patience. You need to be willing to sit and wait for market swings to occur. They are highly unpredictable. Therefore, you need to ready to wait until you reach your desired price points. Otherwise, you may exit the trade before achieving your desired price point.

Use Technical Analysis and Fundamental Analysis

Technical analysis is the use of quantitative tools to analyze price action information. Here, we're talking about price, volatility, and volume. These indicators provide objective data you can use to base your decisions. As a result, you're not basing your investment choices on hunches.

Fundamental analysis is the study of non-quantitative factors that influence price action. These are mainly economic, political, and most importantly, psychological factors. Fundamental analysis is essential when looking at a long-term picture. For example, political decisions by the government influence investors' mindset. Consequently, when investors become uneasy about potential shifts in the market, they may choose to sit on the sidelines. By the same token, if the outlook is positive, you may find investors jumping into the fray. Therefore, a close study of fundamental analysis is essential in any successful swing trading strategy.

To be successful at swing trading, you need to become familiar with both technical analysis and fundamental analysis. Therefore, swing trading requires a greater commitment in terms of time and effort. You need to pay close attention to market conditions. This will enable you to foresee opportunities. When you get really good at spotting future swings, you can make considerable profits.

Advantages of Swing Trading

Let's take a look at the advantages that come with swing trading.

1. Swing trading requires less time than day trading

Even though you need a greater commitment of time and effort in conducting research, the overall amount of time required to engage in swing trading is much less. The reason for this lies in the time it takes to set up trades. In day trading, you need to be at your computer every day, setting up trades, and monitoring your positions.

In the case of swing trading, you set up trades with a longer time frame. Therefore, you won't be placing nearly as many trades. If you plan on doing a combination of day and swing trading, you would still be making fewer trades. Thus, you could conceivably set up trades, and go for days without touching any of your positions. In the meantime, you would be free to continue your research.

2. **Profit maximization**

You stand to make much more profits as you ride large waves as opposed to short-term times. These large waves are the result of capturing significant swings in the market. By spotting these potential swings early on, you can set yourself up for massive gains.

3. **Decisions are based on technical analysis**

In swing trading, technical analysis will tell you what you can expect. While there is certainly a place for hunches, you must base all of your decisions on technical analysis. As such, you'll be able to spot reversals in trend, changes in trading volume, or the emergence of resistance and support levels. Therefore, you need to pay close attention to the fundamentals of technical analysis.

Disadvantages of Swing Trading

Now, let's take a look at the disadvantages that come with swing trading.

1. You are vulnerable to risk

Since you have open positions for longer time frames, you are open to greater risk, particularly with overnight markets. Since developments can occur at any time, you might wake up one morning to a drastically different landscape. Thus, the use of stop-loss triggers is vital to ensuring you don't get wiped out in a single trade.

2. Sudden market reversals

Since markets are relatively unpredictable, any sudden changes can expose you to significant risk. As such, you need to ensure that you are aware of the potential risks. This situation implies that you must use stop-loss or take-profit triggers to ensure that you capture your desired price points.

3. Short-term trends outweigh long-term ones

Even though swing trading has a longer time frame than day trading, it's still a short-term approach. As such, swing traders are more focused on short-term profits rather than long-term ones. This is a necessary approach as swing traders are looking to make as much money as possible in the least amount of time. Since there is no telling what can happen, it's best to cash out as soon as your desired price points are hit.

Are you enjoying this book? If so, i'd be really happy if you could leave a short review on Amazon, it means a lot to me! Thank you!

Chapter 8: How to Succeed at Swing Trading

To be successful at swing trading, you need to become highly familiar with technical analysis. This will be the cornerstone of your strategy. Thus, you must do your homework by consistently checking in on price charts. Based on your observation and analysis, you'll be able to determine what stocks are ripe for the plucking.

However, you don't need to have a crystal ball to figure everything on your own. Lots of investors rely on experts' advice and analysis. You hear these pundits on television or read their columns. They can provide you with insight and knowledge that you may not have been familiar with. As such, it's always good to listen. Nevertheless, always take what they say with a grain of salt.

Mainly, it's important for you to take everything you hear and read and verify the information with your analysis. As a result, you can contrast the opinions you get from the media. Additionally, analytics services like Bloomberg or Market Watch provide an expert recommendation. These analyses are generally available to subscribers only. So, you might want to consider purchasing a subscription. While it is not necessary for you to purchase one, you might want to consider it anyway. The best course of action would be a free trial. That way, you can see if the information is worth the money you would be paying for it.

Swing Trading Strategies

Swing trading strategies require you to dig deeper into the history and trend of price action. This is important as historical data will help you glean into the patterns the stock is trading. When you learn to spot these patterns, you can anticipate what will happen with reasonable accuracy. Anyone who masters technical analysis can predict what will happen. The only thing you need to be aware of is that predict time is nearly impossible. Of course, ballpark estimations are certainly reasonable. However, it's virtually impossible to determine the date and time market shifts will take place. Therefore, you must think twice before believing anyone who claims they can "time" the market.

To make the most of the strategies we will describe herein, please take the time to go over historical data. Most financial news services will provide you with historical data on stock prices. Many will go back at least 10 years. Although, you would only need two or three years' worth of data at most. Going back this far will allow you to determine patterns and trends in stock prices. From there, you will find patterns emerging.

To establish these patterns, you must become familiar with an indicator known as the "moving average."

Moving Average

The moving average is an indicator that is calculated based on historical data. In short, a moving average is the average between the buy and sell price in a given time frame. Depending on the chart, this could be presented on an hourly or daily basis. Some highly specialized real-time charts may present moving average information on a minute-by-minute basis. However, this is not as common as reading hourly data.

Investors and traders use the moving average as a means of determining the overall trend in the price of a stock. Thus, there are three possible types of trends: bearish, bullish, and flat.

A bullish trend means that the price of the stock is rising. While you will find that that chart reflects ups and downs in the overall price action of a stock, the trendline indicates that the price of the stock is rising. Therefore, you can consider this is a bullish trend. Now, it might be impossible to determine how high the price will go. To get an idea, look at previous highs. That should give you an indication of how high the price can go. Unless the stock is experiencing a breakout, you can expect it to fall somewhere around its previous high.

A bearish trend is the opposite of a bullish one. In a bearish trend, the moving average indicates that the price is falling. Hence, you can use this information to either plan an entry point, or stay away from the stock until its price action settles down. Bearish trends usually emerge when the overall trend in the market is down. Nevertheless, individual stocks may fall even though the overall trend in the market is bullish.

A flat or sideways trend means there is no clearly defined trend. As such, it is neither bearish nor bullish. This situation generally indicates that investors are sitting on their hands. In other words, investors are looking to avoid entering the market or selling their positions. This reaction, or lack thereof, is the result of an uncertain situation. When investors don't know what to expect, they may delay making trades as long as possible. To capitalize on a sideways trend, you need to look at the trend leading up to the sideways action. For example, if the trend was bullish, but then it leveled off, you might expect a sharp downturn. In contrast, if the trend was bearish and the leveled off, you might expect a reversal into a bullish one. Unless you have a reasonable belief that the previous trend will continue, the likeliest scenario is that prices will eventually reverse.

10-Day and 20-Day Simple Moving Average

A great tactic swing traders use is called the "simple moving average." This tactic is used as a means of calculating the average daily price of a stock by "smoothing" it out. The term "smoothing" is used in statistics to refer to the process of eliminating fluctuations from a data set. When fluctuations are eliminated, it is possible to see where the overall trend of the data set lies.

To do this, two separate measures are used the 10-day and the 20-day simple moving average. The reason for using these measures lies in using historical data to predict future short-term shifts. Thus, if you want to look at long-term shifts, then you need to look at long-term data such as the 50-day and 200-day moving average.

To produce the simple moving average indicator, all you need to do is add up the average price of the last ten days. After adding them up, divide them by 10. This will give you the average price of the last 10 days. Now, take two separate sets, that is 20 days, and add them together. If you find a divergence between the two indicators, then you have a signal.

A buy signal is sent when the 10-day simple moving average is greater than the 20-day one. This indicates that the price is rising. In contrast, if the 10-day simple moving average is lower than the 20-day one, you must sell. This indicates that the price is heading downward.

You can use this tactic as a means of determining your entry and exits points. Let's assume you don't hold any position. You spot the buy signal, so you set your entry point. Then, you hold until you see the next 10-day moving average cross the

20-day. Once you get the sign to sell, you immediately liquidate your position.

Now, does this mean you have to wait another 10 days before you sell?

No, you don't have to. What you do is you calculate the 10-day moving average every day. All you do is eliminate the 10th day and add the last day. This is why it's called a "moving" average. By doing this, you can spot the exact point in which the price action flashes either a "sell" or "buy" signal.

Moving Average Convergence Divergence Crossover

The moving average convergence divergence (MACD) is commonly used in swing trading to help investors pinpoint when to buy or sell. Unlike the simple moving average, the MACD flashes signals based on two lines, the moving average line (trendline) and the signal line. Most charts represent these are red and blue. Although, you might find any number of color combinations.

The MACD is automatically generated by most stock tracking charts. Also, they are generally available for free. So, you don't need to get an expensive subscription package to have access to these indicators. To take advantage of these indicators, you need to pay attention to the points in which the lines cross one another. This is called a "crossover." Depending on the trend, this will indicate a sell or buy signal.

For instance, when the MACD line crosses over (higher) the signal line, then this indicates the trend is bullish. Therefore, it is a signal to buy. You can also determine this visually as the lines themselves are moving upward. When the MACD line crosses belove (lower) the signal line, then this is a sell line as you can anticipate a bearish trend. Of course, this signal can also be an indication of a "buy" signal if you don't hold an open position. All you have to do is keep an eye on the lines right before the intersect again. This is the lowest price you could buy.

It is important to keep in mind that if you sell after the MACD cross over occurs at the top of the trendline, then you would have missed out on the highest possible returns. Hence, you need to sell right before the lines intersect. This will provide you with the highest possible returns.

Breakout Strategy

The breakout strategy is when you anticipate the price of a stock to blow past its previous highs. To make this strategy work, you need to use the 10-day average to keep a close eye on the stock's overall trend.

Here's how it works.

1. First, identify the trend in the stock of your choice. The trend must be a bullish one. A stock with a bearish trend will not work in this case. If anything, a stock with a bearish trend may break through its floor.

2. Second, look for a double top or triple top pattern. This pattern consists of two or three successive hits upon the stock's upper limit. You must spot at least two hits. If you spot three consecutive hits, then the breakout is imminent.

3. Third, set up your trade. Generally speaking, there is no telling how high the breakout will go. So, it's best to play it safe. You may find that the stock pulls back before continuing to rise. Consequently, you must strive to sell before the pullback.

You can always sell, then buy on the pullback, and sell on the new rise.

4. Lastly, cash out as soon as you see your price point hit. It doesn't matter if the stock continues to rise. It's best to liquate your position before the pullback. Otherwise, your profits may be reduced completely.

With the breakout strategy, you must be aware of the resistance level in the stock. In general, the breakout is imminent when the trading volume dries up. This means that very few trades are being placed compared to the previous volume. The reason for this is generally due to investors expecting a specific action. For example, this action may be government data or some other event.

The most important thing to watch for is greed. Please avoid overriding your take-profit points. There is no telling when the stock's price might pull back. When this happens, the stock may regress before taking off again. Thus, you need to sell before the pullback and then re-enter your position when the stock pulls back. That way, you can capture the new rise.

On the whole, the breakout strategy is the most successful strategy that investors use to make substantial profits. If you can capture a stock at its lowest point, and then ride the wave all the way past the breakout, you are in great shape to make substantial gains. This is the reason why swing trading is all about making patience and timing. Additionally, you must become familiar with technical analysis. Otherwise, it will be very difficult for you to capture the positive swings in the market.

Chapter 9: Fundamentals of Position Trading

Position trading is the longest-term approach in stock trading. This is where investors are willing to lay their money down for a longer time frame in hopes of capturing significant shifts in the market or individual stocks. As a result, position traders don't really care too much about the ups and downs of day-to-day trading. They are more concerned about the big picture. Consequently, position traders are far likelier to look at trades happening in terms of weeks and months rather than days.

It's worth noting that position traders are not passive investors. Passive investors are the ones who employ the "buy and hold" strategy. As such, passive investors simply put their money into an investment and wait for the return at some point. In contrast, position investors are focused on the trend. This approach implies that the trend will lead to the investor's ultimate goal. Therefore, technical analysis and fundamental analysis play a huge role in determining how a trade will be set up.

Understanding Long-Term Trend

In stock trading, any time frame that surpasses a month is considered long-term. In swing trading, it is not surprising to find investors holding their positions for over a month. However, they rarely hold open positions for any period longer than 30 days. Anything after 30 days would fall into the realm of position trading.

The long-term trend is all about identifying where the price of an individual stock may go. This often implies that you need to ride out short-term fluctuations and pullbacks. As a result, you may actually lose value before reaching your ultimate target. This is the reason why position trading is not for investors seeking short-term profits. Position trading is for those who are concerned with truly maximizing their profits.

Typically, position traders aren't overly active. They may place anywhere between 10 to 20 trades per year. However, those trades make should make enough money to offset the time it takes for them to pay off. In the end, position trading provides investors with a lucrative opportunity to cash in on the big picture market shifts.

Advantages of Position Trading

Here are the most significant advantages of position trading

1. ## Position trading doesn't demand much time

Position trading requires upfront planning. However, once the trade is set up, all the investor needs to do is monitor the situation. Once the conditions unfold, the investor can then execute the transaction. Therefore, this trading approach does not require a great deal of time to pursue.

2. ## Profit maximization

Long-term trends generally yield the highest returns. In short-term trading, profit margins can be limited to a few pennies on the dollar. In long-term trading, profits can be several dollars per share. So, when you multiply them over a large number of shares, profits truly add up.

3. ## Risk management

Position trading offers investors the opportunity to manage risk more carefully. In particular, short-term fluctuations are meaningless. Therefore, slight pullbacks are not of concern. As a matter of fact, short-term fluctuations are just a part of the deal. This approach offers greater flexibility. This enables investors to cash out in case they need to leave their position at any time.

Disadvantages of Position Trading

Position trading also has its disadvantages. So, let's take a look at them.

1. Money is tied up for a long time

The duration of trades is the biggest disadvantage of position trading. Some investors are not interested in keeping their money tied up for so long. As such, they would much rather engage in shorter-term deals. This enables them to move their money around, thereby generating smaller, but more consistent profits.

2. There are no guarantees

While position trading offers the possibility of significant returns, there is no guarantee they will materialize. This situation leads investors to think twice about investing their money for any period beyond three or four weeks. Also, it is worth noting that conditions can change overnight. As a result, investors are always exposed to risk.

3. **Opportunity cost**

The term "opportunity cost" refers to the choice you need to make between one thing or another. In this case, you choose to invest in a stock over another. While this is a common decision investors frequently make, investing over a longer time frame magnifies this situation. For instance, investing in a stock for three months means you can't use those funds to trade other stocks throughout that time frame. Thus, your options suddenly become limited. This is the reason why the profits from position trading need to outweigh short-term profits made through day and swing trading.

Combined Strategy

If you consider using position trading as part of a combined strategy, you can truly make your portfolio go into high gear. Hence, you can use position trading as part of a diversified portfolio. For example, you can be a dedicated day trader looking for consistent, short-term gains. Then, you can use swing trading to capitalize on trend reversals and breakouts. Lastly, you can use position trading to capture larger market shifts, especially when you can't quite pinpoint when these shifts will happen.

The main advantage of having a diversified portfolio lies in ensuring that you capture the various time frames the market has to offer. When you have your portfolio spread out over various strategies, you will find that you can make money on a consistent basis.

As for risk, diversification allows you to manage it more effectively. If you place all of your investment capital in a position trading approach, it will be hard for you to make consistent returns. If you neglect long-term market movements, you may miss out on short-term opportunities. Hence, making use of all timeframes helps you capture the bulk of the market's price action.

Lastly, position trading is a great way to invest money, particularly when you are more focused on the big picture. This big-picture approach gives you the opportunity to correct your strategy on the fly. You can enter and exit trades within a reasonable time frame. With short-term investing, you have to roll with the punches. As a result, position trading gives you a higher degree of flexibility as part of your overall strategy.

Chapter 10: How to Succeed at Position Trading

Being successful in position trading is all about anticipating market movements. Since it's impossible to determine the exact moment in which movements will happen, you need to be ready to capitalize at any time. This is the reason why the position remains open for so long. You don't know when prices will go up or down. Nevertheless, you set up your trades so that you're ready for them.

Since you are looking for trends, the main thing is to be ready for the signals that may indicate a reversal. If you are holding a position, you need to be ready for a possible reversal. In this possible reversal, you will get a signal indicating a sale. If you are looking to enter a trade, then a reversal in a bearing trend will indicate your entry point. This is the core strategy around position trading. The issue here is figuring out at what point you need to enter and exit trades.

Like swing trading, position trading uses the moving average as its main technical analysis tool. The difference is that instead of looking at the 10-day or 20-day moving average, we're going to be looking at the 50-day and 200-day moving average.

50-Day and 200-Day Moving Average

These indicators are exactly like the other indicators we discussed earlier. The difference is the time frame they analyze. Analyzing a longer time frame enables you to see the broader trend in a stock. This will help you determine if the price action you have seen is part of the stock's overall trend or not.

For instance, a stock falls sharply in a span of three trading days. On the surface, this movement indicates the stock is in a bearish trend. However, when you look at the 50-day moving average, you can see the stock is actually up. Therefore, this sharp decline is a pullback.

Now, if you are looking to confirm your observations, then you must look at the 200-day moving average. In this indicator, you can confirm the observations from the 50-day moving average. As such, you can confirm the trend or determine it to be the opposite.

Another common situation is steep increases. A stock may show significant increases over a few trading sessions. Yet, the stock is actually down over the 200-day period. Therefore, you can conclude that it's in a bearish trend. The increase in price may simply be the result of market momentum but not a reflection on this stock's true valuation.

These are the observations that you can make when looking at longer time frames. A day trader would not be concerned with these longer-term trends. A day trader would only be interested in seeing the price action over the shorter time frame. As a result, they could capitalize on the fluctuation in the price over one or two trading sessions. Moreover, a swing trader would bank on the movements occurring over three or four trading sessions without really paying much attention to what occurred prior to that.

In position trading, it is important to keep an eye on the big picture. As long as you keep your eyes on the larger scope of the market, you'll be able to spot the potential to make money. So, you should not neglect the way the markets move in addition to individual stocks. This will provide you with the best chance to make serious returns.

Determining Entry and Exit Points

You can use the 50-day and 200-day moving averages in an MACD crossover pattern. In this case, you execute your entry and exit points based on the trendline and the MACD line. When these lines cross over, you can establish your entry and exit points.

Let's consider a bullish trend. In this situation, you have an open position. As such, you are anticipating a climb in the stock's price. You must look at the overall trend, that 200-day moving average, to determine if there is a bullish or bearish trend. Since the 200-day moving average signals a bullish trend, you must wait for the moment in which both lines intersect. At the point in which the 50-day moving average crosses the 200-day moving average, then you have an exit point. This is the point at which you must sell.

At this point, two things can happen. The first thing is a possible trend reversal. The second is a flattening of the trendline. In either case, you stand to see your profit reduced. Thus, you must liquidate your position as close to the intersection point as possible.

In the case of a bearish trend, the point in which the 50-day intersects the 200-day moving average is your optimal entry point. This is the lowest point the stock will hit before bouncing up. As a result, you stand to make the largest profit. If you get into the trade too soon, the price of your stock will fall even further before it rebounds. This situation may cause you to become impatient. Plus, your profit would not be optimal as you could have bought the stock at a lower point. Consequently, you must try your best to get in at the point closest to the intersection of both moving averages.

Pullback and Retracement Strategy

Pullbacks are temporary dips that stocks experience during a bullish trend. Pullbacks can happen for any number of reasons. As such, it's important to look at the overall picture. When you can clearly spot the overall bullish trends, pullbacks provide great opportunities to pick up shares at a cheaper. While the ideal approach is to get in at the lowest point of the trend, you can still capitalize on pullbacks to augment your position.

Position traders use pullbacks all the time to make shorter-term trades, much like swing trading, to generate some additional income while they wait for the big trade to come through. So, these dips in price can provide you with the opportunity to make some immediate profits particularly when you are looking to ride the overall trend.

A retracement is a type of pullback. It is a temporary dip in the price. The difference is that retracements follow a specific pattern. This pattern allows you to determine where the price will fall. Thus, you can plan the points at which you can place additional trades.

The most popular type of retracement strategy is known at the "Fibonacci" retracement. A Fibonacci retracement is based on the classic Fibonacci sequence. When this sequence is applied to a stock chart, you can determine entry and exit points for your trades. Please bear in mind that the overall trend is not expected to change. As such, you are still expecting to ride the wave all the way to the top. Nevertheless, a Fibonacci retracement provides you with the opportunity to plot your movements more accurately.

Here's how it works.

The Fibonacci retracement strategy is based on the Fibonacci sequence of 1, 2, 3, 5, 8, 13, 21, 34,

55, etc. This sequence is present throughout various elements of nature. When applied to stock trading, it enables you to plot specific price points in a chart. Consequently, you can reasonably assume where a price point may be useful to you.

It may seem incredible that stock market fluctuations act according to a similar pattern as the Fibonacci sequence. This is the reason why the Fibonacci retracement strategy is quite useful. Of course, it's not infallible, but produces a lot of positive results most of the time.

The Fibonacci retracement strategy is calculated by placing six lines on a price chart. To do this, you need to take a price chart over any time frame. For the purpose of position trading, you can use a 50-day or 200-day chart. However, you could use a daily chart with hourly price points if you wanted to.

The first two lines correspond to the 100% and 0% levels. The 100% level corresponds to the highest price point in the chart while the 0% corresponds to the lowest. Based on this, you will now plot the 23.6%, 38.2%, 50%, and 61.8% levels. The 50% level corresponds to the exact middle of the chart. Hence, you would add the highest and lowest prices, and then divide them by two. This would give you the exact middle. The 23.6% and 38.2% would represent potential entry points. The 61.8% would be a good exit point. Some investors also like to plot the 75% level as a reference point.

To calculate your entry points, look at how many times the price points intersected at the 23.6% and 38.2% levels. If you find that the price points intersect several times, then you have potential entry points you can rely on. Then, take a look at the 61.8% level as this would be your likeliest exit point.

If you find that none of the points plotted in the Fibonacci retracement strategy intersects with the actual price points in the chart, then you are better off waiting for the overall trend to hit the mark you are expecting. Generally speaking, this is due to a high degree of volatility. Still, Fibonacci retracements are rarely off the mark. So, they can provide you with great reference points.

Resistance Levels and Breakouts

Whenever you experience a breakout, a new resistance level is set. This means that the price of a stock breaks out of its current resistance level and then settles at a higher price point. Therefore, the floor on the stock elevates while a new, much higher resistance level, is set.

This strategy is great because it allows you to determine where new price points can guide your trades. Consider this situation.

A stock currently trading at $11 a share has a support level of $9 and a resistance level of $12. As such, you expect this price to break past the $12 barrier due to technical and fundamental factors. Sure enough, the price bolts past $12 and hits a new high of $15. At this point, you expect the new resistance level to settle somewhere around the $14 to $15 range. After multiple spikes and pullbacks, there are three consecutive hits on the $14.50 mark. Consequently, you determine this to be the new resistance level.

Now, there is also a new support level. This means that the floor of the stock has now been raised from $9 to $11. This is important to note as you now expect the stock's price to hit $11 and then bounce back up. Here, you can use the "triple bottoms" indicator. This is exactly the same as the triple tops. You have three consecutive hits on the floor. This will determine the support level.

At this point, you can now confidently ride a rangebound trading strategy. Since you now have a reasonable belief regarding the range in which the stock will trade, you can place your next trades based on the new floor and ceiling.

This type of approach can be measured by using the 50-day and 200-day moving average. As such, you have enough data to determine how the trade will play out. Considering the length of the trade, you stand to make much more profit as compared to a day trading or swing trading approach.

Please keep in mind that all position trading strategies look to maximize profits based on historical data. If you base your trades on hunches, you may find that the price points you have anticipated may never materialize. Unless you have some reason to believe a stock that has never hit triple digits will do so at some point, then you are better off making your trades based on historical data. While the stock may reach the price point you expect, it may take years to get there. This is the reason why it is better to base your assumptions on real data. Otherwise, you may find yourself with an open position for far too long.

Only blue-chip stocks would be worth holding on to for any period greater than six months. Any other stock may become vulnerable to significant fluctuations. Naturally, this would pose unnecessary risk.

Chapter 11: Value Investing

Professional investors use value investing as a way to make under-the-radar moves. In value investing, investors search for value where others may not see it. Consequently, value investing is all about finding hidden gems.

This investment approach is quite popular among some of the most famous investors in the world. Warren Buffet, Benjamin Graham (Buffet's mentor), Charlie Munger, and David Dodd, among others, have built their investment strategy around value investing.

In essence, value investing consists of finding companies whose market value is below their intrinsic or book value. As such, these are companies that may have fallen on hard times but are poised to rebound at some point. Therefore, you must make an effort to go through financials and price history to determine a company's potential.

Determining Intrinsic Value

A company's intrinsic value is the value of its share capital based on its accounting. This means that a company is really worth what its accounting indicates. What you pay for in the open market is what investors believe it is worth. As such, there is always a difference between both numbers.

To determine a company's intrinsic value, all you need to do is take a company's total share capital and divide it by the number of outstanding shares. For instance, a company's total share value is $1,000,000. There are 100,000 outstanding shares. Therefore, 1,000,000 / 100,000 = 10. This means that each share is worth $10,

A company's intrinsic value changes very little over time. As a matter of fact, it's hard for companies to modify their intrinsic value as there are laws and accounting practices in place that limit this. Therefore, companies must be careful to follow proper accounting principles to ensure they are compliant with laws.

Determining Market Value

At the outset of this book, we explained how a company's market valuation depends on what investors believe the share price is worth. This is the reason why it changes so much in such a short time frame. Therefore, investors determine market value as a result of technical analysis. Of course, there are psychological factors involved. These factors determine whether a stock's valuation rises or falls.

Generally speaking, successful companies have a higher market valuation than intrinsic valuation. This implies that investors are prepared to pay more than the company is truly worth. The reasoning here is based on the company's potential for growth and profit.

When investors feel that a company is not performing up to expectations, its market valuation drops. In such cases, it's valuation may fall below its intrinsic value. In such cases, it could spell the end for the company. In many cases, companies don't rebound. Moreover, they may enter into bankruptcy proceedings. In some cases, companies emerge from restructuring. In others, the company is liquidated.

Spotting Potential Value

Spotting viable candidates for value investing takes time and research. Mainly, you need to pour over the company's financials. When you look at financials, you can get a glimpse into a company's overall health. If the company is generally profitable, but it is going through a tough time, then you can assume the company has a good chance of rebounding. By the same token, if you see bad financials, then the company may be headed for the glue factory.

Also, you must take a look at its price history. To get a good idea of where a company's valuation lies, look at its 200-day moving average. This will provide you with a very clear depiction of the company's true valuation. If you find that it has been in a bearish trend over the 200-day period, then you might be better off looking for another company. However, if you spot a clear moment where the stock took a downward turn, then you might have something.

Setting Up Your Trade

Please note that with value investing, there is no telling how long it will take a company to rebound. While it might take a few weeks, it might take a few months. It all depends on how quickly the company can rebound.

That being said, your entry point should be at the point where you see an MACD cross over. At this point, you will find the trendline crossing over the MACD line. When this happens, you might be on the verge of a trend reversal. Here, you must be ready to jump in and buy.

Next, it's time to determine your exit point. Technically, you could exit at any point above your entry point to make a profit. However, you are looking to maximize your profit. So, a good yardstick for your exit point would be to use the Fibonacci sequence. Look for the 61.8% level. This would be a very good exit point. Realistically, the 100% level may be unattainable, at least in the short term. As such, the 61.8% level would make perfect sense as it's slightly above the halfway mark of the stock's previous high. More conservative investors opt for the 50% level as an exit point.

Now, you can also use Fibonacci retracements to make multiple trades along the way. If the stock successfully rebounds, you can expect multiple pullbacks. Thus, using Fibonacci retracements can help you spot shorter-term trades.

On the whole, it is recommended that you make more conservative assessments. This is not the time to gamble. While it isn't easy to spot companies that might make a rebound, they can be quite profitable deals when you do spot them.

There is one caveat though. Please stay away from the so-called "penny stocks." Penny stocks are companies whose market valuation is less than $5. These are companies that are in liquidation. In the best of cases, they are zombie companies. This term means that they are still moving but not really going anywhere. As such, penny stocks are not worth your time as they will make very little profit if any. You could potentially make very short-term profits with penny stocks. However, it's best to look for companies which a much better chance of rebounding.

Conclusion

Thank you very much for making it all the way to the end of the book. If you're here, then it means you are serious about putting your money to work for you. By investing in the stock market, you are taking a huge step toward achieving your financial goals. As such, you are serious about making money without having to work any harder than you should.

So, what's the next step?

Please go over any sections of this book that you feel you need to review. Please keep in mind that reviewing specific parts of this book will help you improve your knowledge and experience. As you gain more and more experience, you'll be able to make the most of the information you have learned in this book.

It is also important to consider the options you have available to you. Often, it is not easy to make decisions given the vast array of options out there. This is the reason why it's important to ensure that you have all the information you need before making investment decisions. Moreover, please make sure that is careful with the so-called "gurus" and "experts." Thus, it is vital that you always verify the claims these individuals make. With this book, you can safely determine if the claims you hear are true or not.

The time has come for you to get started on the most exciting journey of your life. Stock market investing is the best way you can achieve your financial hopes and dreams. So, do take the time to carefully make your investment plan. As you set up your goals and aims, you will find that being realistic is the best place to start. As you gain more experience, you can set more ambitious goals. In the end, the sky is the limit when it comes to investing in the stock market.

Thank you once again for your time and dedication in reading this book. If you have found the information herein useful and informative, please tell your friends, colleagues, and family about it. They too will find this book to be useful.

They will appreciate your sharing this information.

One last thing...

Stock market investing requires investors to do their homework. Please take the time to become familiar with technical analysis and fundamental analysis. The information you get from doing careful research will help you make the best possible investment decision. The good thing is that most of this research is done for you. Therefore, getting access to this information (usually through a subscription service) will help you make the most of the investment decisions you make. Often, spending a few extra dollars a month will make the difference between winning and losing trades.

Now that you're all set to go, please don't forget to have fun. In the end, if you enjoy investing, you will fare much better. By enjoying the time you spend investing, you will make much more money than you could have ever imagined!

If you enjoyed this book, please let me know your thoughts by leaving a short review on Amazon.

Thank you!